South West Coast Path
Coastal **Pub Walks:** Dorset

Part of the England Coast Path

Text: *Fiona Barltrop*

Series editor: *Tony Bowerman*

Photographs: *Fiona Barltrop, Tony Bowerman, Alamy, Adobe Stock, Dreamstime, Shutterstock*

Design: *Carl Rogers and Laura Hodgkinson*

© Northern Eye Books Limited 2019

Fiona Barltrop has asserted her rights under the Copyright, Designs and Patents Act, 1988 to be identified as the author of this work. All rights reserved.

This book contains mapping data licensed from the Ordnance Survey with the permission of the Controller of Her Majesty's Stationery Office. © Crown copyright 2019. All rights reserved. License number 100047867

Northern Eye Books

ISBN 978-1-908632-87-6

A CIP catalogue record for this book is available from the British Library.

Printed in the UK
www.northerneyebooks.co.uk

First published in 2019 by:

Northern Eye Books Limited
Northern Eye Books, Tattenhall, Cheshire CH3 9PX

tony@northerneyebooks.com

www.northerneyebooks.co.uk

 @northerneyebooks

 @northerneyeboo

For sales enquiries, please call 01928 723 744

www.englandcoastpath.co.uk

Cover: *The Anchor Inn, Seatown, (Walk 2)*

Contents

South West Coast Path

Running for 630 miles from Minehead in Somerset, around the tip of Land's End and back to South Haven Point at the mouth of Poole Harbour in Dorset, the South West Coast Path is Britain's longest National Trail. Bordered by the Bristol and English channels and looking out to the open Atlantic, it encompasses some of England's most spectacular and wildest coastline, where the diversity of plant, animal and insect life can be stunning. The seas, coves and surrounding hinterland have been a dramatic setting for a gloriously rich history, which has inspired countless tales of romance, drama and intrigue.

This series of Top Ten Walks explores highlights along the way; showcasing the coast's natural beauty, wildlife and heritage and stimulating the imagination. Who knows, you may be inspired to come back to tackle the complete trail.

Summer music festival at the 'Square & Compass', Worth Matravers

Pubs along the Dorset Coast

The excellent pubs to be found along Dorset's coast well complement the walking to be had along this superlative stretch of the South West Coast Path. The Dorset and East Devon coast — known as the 'Jurassic Coast' — is England's first natural World Heritage Site. It covers 95 miles of stunning coastline, with rocks recording 185 million years of earth's history, spanning the Triassic, Jurassic and Cretaceous periods. These are laid out from the oldest to the youngest moving west to east. The pub walks here are also ordered from west to east, starting with Lyme Regis and finishing at Studland. All the pubs are situated either right on the coast or a short distance inland and almost every one is open all day.

"I must go down to the seas again, to the lonely sea and the sky...."

John Masefield, poet

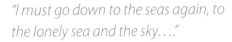

TOP 10 **Walks:** Dorset's best coastal Pub Walks

EACH OF THE SELECTED CIRCULAR WALKS incorporates a stretch of the South West Coast Path, with most starting and finishing close to a superb pub. Combined they cover the very best stretches of Dorset's coastline, one of great natural beauty and variety. Needless to say, tourist honeypots like Lulworth Cove can get very busy, especially in peak season, but once away from the car parks you can always escape the crowds on the Coast Path. With the pubs open all year and the walking good in all seasons, Dorset's coast is a year-round destination.

Harbour Inn
Lyme Regis
page 8

Anchor Inn
Seatown
page 14

Ilchester Arms
Abbotsbury
page 20

Pulpit Inn
Portland Bill
page 26

The Harbour Inn sits right on the beach

Harbour Inn
Lyme Regis

Distance/time: 9 kilometres / 5½ miles. Allow 3 - 4 hours

Start: Holmbush car park, Pound Street (A3052 west side of Lyme Regis)

Grid ref: SY 337 920

Ordnance Survey map: Explorer 116 (Lyme Regis & Bridport)

The Pub: The Harbour Inn, 23 Marine Parade, Lyme Regis DT7 3JF | 01297 442299 | www.harbourinnlymeregis.co.uk

Walk outline: Historic Lyme Regis is well worth exploring at the end of the walk. Landslides are common along this stretch of coastline, and the Coast Path east of Lyme Regis has been diverted inland, while to the west it runs through dense woodland for several miles, with no exit routes. So the walk heads inland through the countryside to Uplyme, passing beneath an impressive viaduct and returning beside the River Lim into town.

There are numerous places at which to eat and drink in Lyme Regis. Situated on the beach front overlooking the Cobb and Lyme Bay, the Harbour Inn, a family owned pub/restaurant, is one to try, recommended for its location, food and service.

Beach tables

▶ The Harbour Inn at a glance

Open: Daily from 11am
Brewery/company: Free house
Ales and wine: Selection of local ales including Otter Ale, plus extensive wine list
Food: Home-cooked food served noon-2.30pm and 6–9pm, cream teas 3-6pm. Specials board and evening events menus
Outside: Tables on veranda and alfresco dining on private beach area
Children & dogs: Children's menu and smaller portions of one or two main dishes available. Dogs welcome in bar area

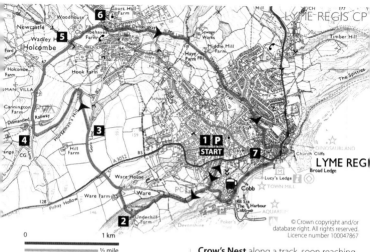

0   1 km

½ mile

The Walk

1. Head to the far end of the **car park** and continue along private **Pine Walk**, then follow a path to the National Trust's **'Ware Cliffs'**, where you'll reach a fingerpost and junction at a gate. Go through the gate and keep ahead, joining the **South West Coast Path**. (Down to the left the Coast Path descends through woods to a car park and the Cobb harbour, the route by which you will return at the end of the walk).

In the next field continue on the Coast Path at a signed four-way junction, with fine coastal views looking back. Just before reaching a house (Crow's Nest) you enter Devon. Bear left at the

Crow's Nest along a track, soon reaching the Axmouth-Lyme Regis **Undercliffs National Nature Reserve**. Carry on ahead (ignoring a permissive footpath to Chimney Rock that forks right) and follow the track to a turning on the right signed for 'Chimney Rock and Ware Lane'.

2. Leaving the Coast Path, turn right up steps to **Chimney Rock**. Cross the stile and go across the field. The path leads to **Ware Farm Manor** drive and **Ware Lane**. Turn left to the **A3052**. Cross and continue along **Gore Lane** for 500 metres, passing a turning on the left for Hill Farm.

3. Fork left along a field edge, then descend to a lane. Turn left and carry on along the lane below Horseman's Hill.

Thatched watermill in the Lim Valley

Pass to the right of the cottage at the end continuing along a bridleway. Beyond a gate is your first view of **Cannington viaduct** down to the right. *This disused railway viaduct, comprising ten arches of concrete, carried the Axminster and Lyme Regis Light Railway (1903 – 1965).* Walk down the field to the road.

4. Turn right along **Cannington Lane** going underneath the viaduct. Keep ahead at a junction ignoring the turning on the left. At the next junction, as the lane curves right, fork left. At the crossroads keep ahead on an access road.

5. Fork right at a public footpath sign, joining the route of the **East Devon Way**, waymarked with a foxglove. Follow the path down the grass to **Uplyme**, keeping ahead across a **footbridge** past the **cricket club** and **village hall** to the road.

6. Turn right and very shortly, on reaching the **Talbot Arms** car park, turn left, still following the **East Devon Way**, signed for 'Lyme Regis 1½' [miles]. Cross the next road and carry on along the path which follows the **River Lim valley** back to the centre of **Lyme Regis**. The path leads through trees to another road.

Summer visitors exploring the famous Cobb at Lyme Regis

Cross and continue along **Mill Lane** opposite to a thatched cottage and thence along the path, which leads down to the thatched **Old Mill**. *There were seven mills in the Lim valley in the 18th century, of which this is one, now a house.*

At a junction, cross the footbridge over the **River Lim**, then continue across the field and over the **Lim** again. The path enters a wooded area and then joins an access road, continuing with the river on the right. Keep straight on at **Horn Bridge**, now on a road called **Windsor Terrace**. Cross another road and carry on until the road slopes down to the **river** and a ford. Cross the **footbridge**

and carry on to the next road (**Mill Green**), following it round to a road junction. Keep ahead crossing the road to continue along the **surfaced path** (signed 'Riverside Walk') with the **River Lim** on your right and the **mill leat** on the left.

7. This leads to the **Town Mill** where there's a working watermill (the mill site dates to 1340), art galleries and creative artisans — well worth a visit. Follow **Mill Lane** uphill, right into **Coombe Street** and immediately left along **Monmouth Street** towards the **church**. At the T-junction cross the road, turn left then right through the **churchyard** to the far

end where there's a superb view along the cliffs and coastline to the east/south-east, with the sea wall below. A path leads down to it. Turn left to extend the walk eastwards to the end of the **sea wall;** otherwise turn right and make your way along the **seafront** to the **Cobb harbour** and **car park** beyond. Turn right at the **Coast Path** sign back uphill to the top (Ware Cliffs) and retrace your initial steps to the start to complete the walk. ◆

Lyme Undercliff

Between Lyme Regis and Seaton, the Coast Path runs through the Undercliff, an atmospheric wilderness of woodland and dense scrub formed by landslips. Notable was a massive cliff fall in1839 known as the Great Landslip. Today, the area is protected as a National Nature Reserve, important for its geology and wildlife, and is one of the largest active coastal landslide systems in Western Europe. Despite the lack of sea views and escape routes, it's an experience to walk through it.

The Anchor Inn is tucked below Golden Cap at Seatown

Anchor Inn
Seatown

What to expect:
Good paths and tracks over grassy cliff top terrain; quite strenuous with several ascents and descents

Distance/time: 10.75 kilometres / 6¾ miles. Allow 4 hours

Start: Beach car park, Seatown

Grid ref: SY 420 917

Ordnance Survey map: Explorer 116 (Lyme Regis & Bridport)

The Pub: Anchor Inn, Seatown, Bridport DT6 6JU | 01297 489215 | www.theanchorinnseatown.co.uk

Walk outline: Beginning from the Anchor Inn car park, the outward leg follows a splendid stretch of the Coast Path westwards to Stonebarrow Hill, east of Charmouth. The ascent of Golden Cap at the start of the walk is rewarded by far-reaching views. More ups and downs follow. The return leg passes a ruined medieval chapel, all that remains of the once thriving hamlet of Stanton St Gabriel.

The Anchor Inn is a multi-award-winning pub situated in a beautiful location above the beach tucked away at the end of a no-through lane. There is excellent walking along in the Coast Path in either direction, with spectacular views.

Summer on the patio

▶ The Anchor Inn at a glance

Open: Daily 10am–11pm

Brewery/company: Palmers Brewery

Ales and wine: Varied selection of real ales from Palmers in Bridport; good choice of wines including local Dorset ones; variety of cocktails

Food: Award-winning menu includes fresh fish and produce from local suppliers. Food served noon-9pm

Accommodation: Three stylish 'boutique' bedrooms

Outside: Tables on patio and grassy cliff-top area

Children & dogs: Both welcome

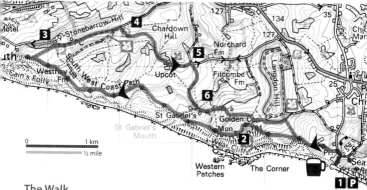

The Walk

1. Exit the **car park** and turn right along the lane, passing the turning on the right for the holiday park, and continue to a **Coast Path fingerpost** pointing left, about 200 metres from the car park. The route to Golden Cap is well waymarked. (The symbol for the Coast Path, as for all National Trails, is the acorn, used on the fingerposts.) The terrain is part of the **National Trust's Golden Cap estate**. A long steady ascent up the grass with some steps to finish with leads you to the **trig point** on the **summit plateau**, at 191metres/627 feet the highest point along the southern coastline of Britain.

On clear days the view extends from Portland in the east to Start Point in the west. Also on the summit is a memorial to the Earl of Antrim, chairman of the National Trust in the 1960s and 1970s. It was he who spearheaded its 1965 fundraising campaign, named Enterprise Neptune, to purchase stretches of unspoiled coastline, thereby saving them from development. The Golden Cap Estate was part of this, parcels of land being added in stages over the years. Of the 780 miles of coastline now in the care of the National Trust, three quarters has been acquired since the launch of the campaign, now called the Neptune Coastline Campaign. The majority of donations have been gifts left in wills.

2. From the summit head down the zigzagging path to a kissing gate and junction, continuing on the **Coast Path** down the grassy slopes. The path descends through vegetation to cross a **footbridge** over a **stream** above St

The ruins of 13th-century St Gabriel's Chapel

Gabriel's Mouth, and thereafter t**wo more footbridges** are crossed — over **Ridge Water** and then **Westhay Water**.

The Coast Path heads on uphill to a junction where you bear left (signed 'Charmouth and NT car park'). At the next junction by a fence and gate, the Coast Path turns right, diverted from its former ongoing route due to land slippage. Follow the path alongside the fence keeping ahead at a four-way junction to the **National Trust car park** on **Stonebarrow Hill**.

From up here Golden Cap can be seen to the south-east, with Portland to its right in the far distance.

3. Turn right along the track passing some **information panels** on the right and the small **National Trust shop** (housed in an old radar station) on the left, where refreshments are available (open from Easter to the end of October, volunteer availability and weather permitting). Continue along the track/bridleway, signed for 'Chardown Hill', to reach another **car park** and path junction.

Looking back down to Seatown from the top of Golden Cap

4. Fork right along the bridleway signed 'To Coast Path East, Chardown Hill, Golden Cap'. Go through a gate and take the right fork down the grass: no clear path initially, but before long an obvious track is joined. Ignoring turnings, follow the track to **Upcot Farm**, bending left through the farm to continue on the track/rough access road, passing a footpath turn on the right.

5. At the next junction (**Pickaxe Cross**), turn right down the access road for St Gabriel's. Follow the road to **St Gabriel's House**, an 18th-century manor house, now divided into National Trust holiday cottages.

6. *As described in the* **National Trust information panel** *nearby, this secluded valley was the location of the former hamlet of Stanton St Gabriel, dating back to the 11th century. By the 18th century the settlement was all but abandoned, the residents having left to work in the mills and rope-walks of Bridport.*

Continuing on the bridleway you'll pass the ruins of the 13th century **St Gabriel's Chapel**, *used as a warehouse for smugglers in the 19th century*. Keep ahead where a footpath forks right (uphill towards Golden Cap). A little further on the bridleway turns right up the northern slopes of **Golden Cap**, and then left,

signed for 'Langdon Wood'. At the next junction bear right along the bridleway signed for 'Langdon Hill'. Continue on the bridleway along the southern edge of the **Langdon Hill woodland** — fine coastal views to your right. At the next fork bear right, signed 'Seatown, To Coast Path', heading downhill to rejoin the outward route. Retrace your steps back to the start to complete the walk. ♦

Fossil collecting

The Jurassic Coast is world famous for its geology and fossils, which can be found at many locations along the Dorset coast, including Seatown and Charmouth. A voluntary code of conduct operates: collecting from the beach is acceptable but digging into the cliffs is not. The Charmouth Heritage Centre is a good place to learn more about what fossils to look out for and where; or you can join an organised fossil hunting walk.

The Ilchester Arms is a lovely 17th-century coaching inn in Abbotsbury

Ilchester Arms
Abbotsbury

What to expect:
Grassy downland paths, shingle beach

Distance/time: 10 kilometres / 6½ miles. Allow 3½ hours

Start: Village car park in Rodden Row on B3157

Grid ref: SY 578 852

Ordnance Survey map: OS Explorer OL15 (Purbeck & South Dorset)

The Pub: The Ilchester Arms, 9 Market St, Abbotsbury, Weymouth DT3 4JR | 01305 873841 | www.theilchester.co.uk

Walk outline: Set amidst downland behind Chesil Beach, Abbotsbury is one of the most interesting villages in Dorset. The outward leg leads along a ridge-top path via the Iron Age hillfort of Abbotsbury Castle — with excellent views all the way — then heads down to the coast to return alongside Chesil Beach. A short detour at the end climbs to St Catherine's Chapel and one of the loveliest viewpoints.

The Ilchester Arms is a 17th-century coaching inn situated in the centre of the village. Abbotsbury's other pub, the Swan Inn, is worth trying, too. There's also a choice of teashops including the Old Schoolhouse Tearooms with a delightful walled garden, opposite the Ilchester Arms.

Eat in the sunny conservatory

▶ The Ilchester Arms at a glance

Open: Fri –Sat: 11am-midnight, Sun-Thurs: 11am-10pm
Brewery/company: Ei Group (formerly Enterprise)
Ales and wine: Doom Bar and guest ales; good selection of wines.
Food: Home-made food using fresh local produce; lunch, evening and children's menus. Food available noon-2.15pm, 6—8.45pm
Accommodation: 9 en-suite bedrooms, including two dog-friendly ones
Outside: Conservatory, patio and garden with views towards St Catherine's Chapel
Children & dogs: Children and well-behaved dogs welcome

The Walk

1. Exit the **car park** by the main entrance, cross the road and walk along **Rosemary Lane** opposite. Turn left at the T-junction along **Back Street** for a very short distance. Turn right beside a small **thatched cottage** along a track signed to 'Blind Lane, Hill Fort 1¾, Hardy Mon 3½'. Follow the **bridleway** uphill, going through a gate and continuing across open grassland. Looking back there are fine views over Abbotsbury village with the church, tithe barn and St Catherine's Chapel on the hill-top visible, the Fleet lagoon beyond. Bear left at the first junction, signed for the 'Hill Fort 1½'. Go through another gate and keep ahead across the grass to a third gate and fingerpost, bearing left along the track to the top of the ridge.

2. The broad grassy ridge-top path, which provides excellent views over the coast and inland, is part of the waymarked **South Dorset Ridgeway**, *a 17-mile route which links West Bexington with Osmington Mills. It was previously called the Inland Coast Path, and indeed it is still an official alternative route for the corresponding coastal stretch of the South*

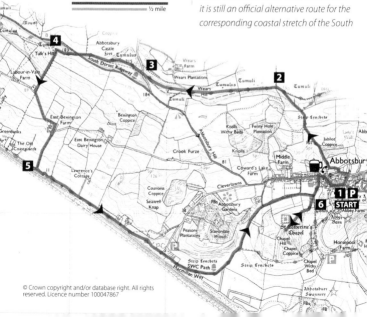

Abbotsbury sits in a fold of the downs

West Coast Path. Running parallel to the coast and at a varying distance inland, it's a fine walk in its own right, providing extensive coastal views.

3. Having crossed a minor road you reach **Abbotsbury Castle** (hill fort), its earthworks clearly visible. It is unusual for its triangular shape. From the **trig point**, a splendid viewpoint, carry on along the **South Dorset Ridgeway** to the **B3157**. Cross and go through a gate beside the National Trust **Tulk's Hill sign**. Continue alongside the wall to its corner and a waymark post.

4. Turn left down the footpath signed for Chesil Beach, descending past some bushes and along the edge of a field passing to the left of a house near **Labour-in-Vain Farm**. Cross a stile and head diagonally across the field down towards **East Bexington Farm**. Continue on a track past the **farm buildings** and then down the edge of the field to the coast.

5. Now on the **Coast Path**, turn left along a tarmac lane which runs behind Chesil Beach. *This great 28 kilometre/18 mile-long shingle bank stretches from West*

Chesil Beach stretches for 18 miles between West Bay and Portland

Bay to Portland. The pebbles are graded in size by the waves, the smallest being at the far western end. Between Abbotsbury and Portland the beach is separated from the mainland by the Fleet lagoon.

When the road turns inland past a **car park**, continue along the shingle, hedge on the left. Before long the Coast Path curves inland.

At a fingerpost where the 'Swannery and Coast Path' are signed to the right, keep ahead along the bridleway, signed for 'Abbotsbury', which takes you round the west and north of **Chapel Hill**. Ignore the first two turnings on the left.

6. At a junction where the track bends left to the village, turn right to follow the signed path up the grass to **St Catherine's Chapel**, and enjoy good views back over the village as you ascend.

Built in the late 14th century by Abbotsbury Abbey, the chapel was dedicated to St Catherine of Alexandria, and may have been a place of pilgrimage. It survived the Dissolution of the Abbey probably because of its importance as a beacon to seafarers. Constructed entirely of stone, the walls are some four feet thick.

Retrace your steps and continue along **Chapel Lane** to **Market Street**, turning

right back to the **car park** to complete the walk. ♦

Close to the car park are St Nicholas Church, built in the late 14th or early 15th century, the scant remains of the Abbey (the gable end of a building) and down the paved path the great thatched tithe barn (now part of the Children's Farm), probably built in the 14th century, too.

Abbotsbury and its Swannery

The Benedictine Abbey of St Peter was built in the 11th century, growing in wealth and influence over the following centuries, but that came to an end under Henry VIII when it was destroyed in the Dissolution of the monasteries. Stone from the abbey was used in many buildings in the village. Only the chapel and tithe barn were left unharmed. The famous Swannery was established by the monks who farmed the swans for food.

The recently refurbished Pulpit Inn on Portland Bill

Pulpit Inn
Portland Bill

What to expect:
Easy walking on cliff-top Coast Path, inland paths and tracks beside fields

Distance/time: 7.25 kilometres / 4½ miles. Allow 2½ hours

Start: Cheyne Weares car park, Southwell Road, Portland

Grid ref: SY 693 704

Ordnance Survey map: OS Explorer OL15 (Purbeck & South Dorset)

The Pub: The Pulpit Inn, Portland Bill, Southwell, Portland DT5 2JT | 01305 821237 | www.thepulpitinnportland.co.uk

Walk outline: Portland is unlike anywhere else in Dorset. Portland Bill at the southernmost tip is the focus of this walk, which starts from a car park (noted for its fine view) on the east side of the Island, and follows the Coast Path clockwise round the Bill, cutting across inland to return to the start. For those with the time and energy, a complete circuit of Portland is recommended (see longer alternative).

Situated about 500 metres north of Portland Bill and close to the route of the Coast Path, the Pulpit Inn — which was refurbished and given a new lease of life by the present owner — makes an ideal refreshment stop for walkers.

Fresh local seafood

▶ The Pulpit Inn at a glance

Open: 11am-2/3pm, weekdays; 11am-4pm, weekends; 6pm-8/9pm, Sat evening. Times may vary - ring to confirm
Brewery/company: Free house
Ales and wine: Real ales include Doom Bar and Ringwood. Choice of wines
Food: Available during opening hours. Good selection of dishes (starters, main menu and desserts, including children's menu). Fresh local seafood includes Portland crab. Specials board and Sunday carvery
Accommodation: Two en-suite B&B rooms with sea views
Outside: Patio with picnic tables and panoramic views of Portland Bill
Children & dogs: Both welcome

Portland Bill

cottages available as holiday lets.

The **Coast Path** passes a large collection of **wooden huts** and another **derrick** used by fishermen. Just beyond that is the **Lobster Pot restaurant** and **Portland Bill lighthouse**, where there is a **Visitor Centre**.

2. Carry on past the lighthouse to the obelisk. *North-west of the obelisk is the famous Pulpit Rock, the remains of a natural rock arch with a large slab of rock leaning against it.*

The **Coast Path** bears inland from Pulpit Rock to skirt a fenced off **MoD site**. Returning to the coast, the path continues along the grassy cliff-top passing the National Coastwatch Institution **lookout station** and the **Higher Lighthouse**. *The sheer cliffs ahead await those walking the full circuit of Portland.*

3. About 400 metres from the lookout station, turn right at a **stone marker** above **Wallsend Cove** and follow a wide grassy path, wall on left, soon bending right and then left, now on a defined track. As this curves right keep ahead on another, which becomes a walled, then hedged track.

The Walk

1. Exit the **car park** and turn left along the pavement opposite passing the turning for **Coombefield quarry**. Soon cross the road again and fork left down a track, signposted for the 'Coast Path'. The path leads through **disused coastal quarries**, passing a **wooden derrick** (crane) once used for lowering stone into barges.

Looking inland as you get closer to Portland Bill you can see the two older lighthouses, which the current operational one replaced in the early 20th century. The nearer Lower Lighthouse, is now a bird observatory while the Higher Lighthouse, situated on the west coast, is privately owned, its adjoining

Jurassic limestone underlies the Isle of Portland

4. On reaching a tarmac lane, turn right through the kissing gate and continue beside fields, gradually descending to join the road. Turn left alongside the road and take the next footpath on the right past another **disused quarry** to rejoin the **Coast Path**. Turn left and retrace your steps to the start to complete the walk. ♦

Longer alternative circuit: 13 kilometres/8 miles. Allow 4 - 4½ hours

Start from the **New Ground parking area**, close to the **Heights Hotel**, on the summit of the Isle (grid ref: SY 690 731)

The view from here is the best on Portland, taking in Lyme Bay, Chesil Beach, Portland harbour and the mainland.

The route is straightforward: you simply turn left and follow the waymarked Coast Path clockwise. Information panels describe the many points of interest.

Portland stone

Portland stone, a type of limestone, has been extensively used as a building material over the centuries, especially after the Great Fire of London. Many major public buildings such as St Paul's Cathedral are constructed of it and likewise the now redundant Trinity House Obelisk at Portland Bill, built in 1844 to warn ships of a low shelf of rock which extends south into the sea. Like all of Portland, the area around Portland Bill has been shaped by quarrying.

The charming Smugglers Inn at Osmington Mills

Smugglers Inn
Osmington Mills

What to expect:
*Undulating coast path,
low cliffs, steady ascent to
top of high chalk cliffs, field
and woodland paths*

Distance/time: 9.5 kilometres / 6 miles. Allow 3 hours

Start: Smugglers Inn, Osmington Mills car park (customers only) or roadside nearby; alternatively, if busy, Ringstead Bay car park, pt 2 (charge), or NT car park above Ringstead Bay, pt 6 (free)

Grid ref: SY 735 817

Ordnance Survey map: OS Explorer OL15 (Purbeck & South Dorset)

The Pub: Smugglers Inn, Osmington Mills, Weymouth DT3 6HF | 01305 833125 | www.smugglersinnosmingtonmills.co.uk

Walk outline: Heading westwards from Osmington Mills, the outward leg follows the Coast Path along low cliffs to Ringstead Bay, continuing uphill past a wooden chapel onto higher cliffs. Beyond is the chalk headland of White Nothe with splendid views. Heading back, the walk bears inland to a National Trust car park on the Downs, then drops past South Down Farm to return via paths parallel to the coast.

Dating back to the 13th century, and later used as a smugglers' haunt, the welcoming Smugglers Inn is right on the Coast Path. The partly thatched pub is large but cosy with wooden beams, log fires, and picnic tables in the attractive beer garden.

Thatched doorway

▶ **The Smugglers Inn at a glance**

Open: Mon-Fri 11am-11pm, Sat 10am-11pm, Sun 10am-10:30pm
Brewery/company: Hall & Woodhouse
Ales and wine: Good selection of Badger beers; wide choice of wines
Food: Excellent menu with plenty of choice, including: Steak and Tangle Foot Pie and Badger Beer battered fish and chips; specials board with seasonal dishes; Sunday roasts. Children's menu
Food served noon-9pm; brunch at weekends 10am-3pm
Accommodation: Four en-suite bedrooms
Children & dogs: Both very welcome **Outside:** Extensive beer garden

The Walk

1. Head down to the **Smugglers Inn** and go round the left hand side of it. The surfaced path leads to a gate into a field. Carry on ahead to a kissing gate and continue along the **Coast Path**, fence on left. After wet weather, this path can be quite muddy. The Isle of Portland is clearly in view to the south. The path leads past a couple of **Second World War lookouts** and the **site of the abandoned medieval village of West Ringstead** (a series of earthworks on private land). A mile from the start the path joins a track leading past dwellings on the Ringstead Estate.

2. The official route of the **Coast Path** carries on along the tarmac, following the access road round to the left

which leads to the **car park** and **kiosk**, although the **Coast Path** turns right just before, continuing behind the **caravan park**.

But the more **scenic alternative** is to follow the track round to the right and go down the ramp to the **shingle beach** (sand at low tide) — good for swimming. *Ahead of you in the distance is the White Nothe headland.* Walk along the beach to a flight of **wooden steps.** Ascend these and head diagonally across the grass to rejoin the **Coast Path**, bearing right along the track.

3. At the first footpath junction you reach, signed 'NT South Down' to the left, cross the stile to make a **brief detour** to view the nearby **bunker** that was part

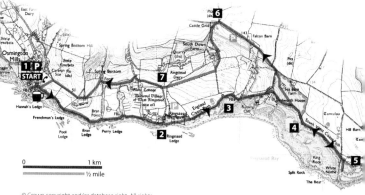

Fossil-rich grey-white limestone cliffs to the east of Osmington Mills

of the former radar station called **RAF Ringstead**. *An information panel provides more details.*

Return to the **Coast Path** and continue up through blackthorn scrub joining a track which becomes an access road leading to the **wooden chapel of St Catherine's by the Sea**, a peaceful place with lovely views from the **churchyard** and **benches** on which to rest. Just past the chapel, the **Coast Path** continues on the road, but the more direct route is to fork right along the footpath. Rejoining the **Coast Path** very shortly at the next junction (the drive to Holworth House) go through the kissing gate and up the grass ahead to the top of the high chalk cliffs.

4. Go through another kissing gate to continue along the top, fence on left. *Below is the huge **undercliff**, formed by landslides. The section called Burning Cliff to the west is so-named after a landslip in 1826 caused oil in the shale to set alight and smoulder for many years. Looking back there are fine views of the coastline stretching round Weymouth Bay and out to Portland.*

Walkers approaching the summit of White Nothe

5. When you reach the former **Coastguard Cottages** at **White Nothe** (meaning White Nose) turn right along a path out onto the headland, where a **World War Two pillbox-cum-lookout** is sited. Carry on past this and a **stone marker** just beyond (indicating the steep hazardous Smugglers Path that descends from here) to reach a **stone bench** a little further on. From here there's a fine view along the chalk cliffs to the east. Retrace your steps to Point 4 enjoying the views over Ringstead Bay. Go through the kissing gate and head across the grass, on National Trust land, towards **Sea Barn Farm**, passing either side of it and exiting the field via a stile at the far corner, to a

junction of tracks. Keep ahead to the **NT Ringstead Bay car park** (information panels).

6. Turn left down the road to **South Down Farm**, continuing on a track past the buildings. Then turn right along a footpath heading down the field — there's no defined path, but waymarker posts indicate the route. After crossing a **footbridge** the path meets the road.

7. Turn right along the road and take the next footpath (access road) on the left, passing **Woodlands Cottage** on the right. Continue along the track into **woodland**, curving right past a gate and ignoring turns to the left. At the

three-way junction bear left signed for 'Osmington Mills', heading up the grass towards dwellings. Continue along the lane (good views) for 350 metres. At a gate on the left cross the stile beside it and head on down the grass back to **Osmington Mills** to complete the walk. ♦

Smugglers' coast?

Smuggling was rife along the Dorset coast in the past, especially during the 18th and early 19th centuries — as names like Smugglers Inn and Smugglers Path attest. The former was the headquarters of the French smuggler Pierre Latour and one of the main landing places for smuggled goods, while the latter, a path which zig-zags steeply down from the top of the White Nothe headland is said to have been the escape route described in the 19th-century children's novel Moonfleet.

A summery mural decorates the popular Lulworth Cove Inn

Lulworth Cove Inn
Lulworth Cove

What to expect:
Strenuous outward leg, some steep ups and downs, good paths; easier, more level return

Distance/time: 10.5 kilometres / 6½ miles. Allow 4 hours

Start: Lulworth Cove car park (charge)

Grid ref: SY 822 800

Ordnance Survey map: OS Explorer OL15 (Purbeck & South Dorset)

The Pub: Lulworth Cove Inn, Main Road, Wareham BH20 5RQ | 01929 400333 | www.lulworth-coveinn.co.uk

Walk outline: From Lulworth Cove the route heads up Hambury Tout and dips to Durdle Door, before running along rollercoaster-like, grassy, chalk cliffs. Before reaching White Nothe, the walk heads back along inland paths, along the northern flank of Hambury Tout and then back down to the car park. At the end, there's a short stroll to Lulworth Cove and Stair Hole.

Situated right on the doorstep of Lulworth Cove, the historic Inn is ideally located for this stunning stretch of Dorset's coastline. The decor is light and contemporary, with a suitably coastal colour scheme of pastel blues and whites, and wood burners for winter. The staff are hospitable and helpful.

Painted pub sign

▶ **The Lulworth Cove Inn at a glance**

Open: Mon-Sun: 11am-10:30pm
Brewery/company: Hall & Woodhouse
Ales and wine: Locally brewed Badger beers and extensive wine list
Food: Eclectic menu with plenty of choice, regularly changing seasonal specials, Sunday roasts and vegan, vegetarian and gluten free options. Children's menu — up to the age of 10. Food served noon-9pm
Accommodation: 12 en-suite rooms, most with sea views (no pets)
Children & dogs: Both very welcome **Outside:** Large attractive terrace

The chalk cliffs at Swyre Head with Bat's Head beyond

The Walk

1. From the far end of the **car park** follow the wide **stone-pitched track** uphill which offers fine views back over Lulworth Cove as you ascend. At the top the track levels out and then bends right (a new path from the original, still shown on the OS map) to reach a junction near the **Durdle Door Holiday Park**. Bear left to continue down the track to **Durdle Door**, the **Man o' War Cove** below on the eastern side of the headland. *The famous rock arch is to be seen from the western side. No matter how many pictures you've seen of Durdle Door — among the*

most photographed landmarks of the Jurassic Coast — there's nothing like seeing it with your own eyes, all the better without the crowds.

2. Continuing westwards the **Coast Path** descends to the memorably named dry valley of **Scratchy Bottom** (the latter word often used for a valley, while the former may refer to rough undergrowth), then heads steeply up **Swyre Head**, which affords a splendid view looking back shortly before the summit. *This is, in fact, one of two Swyre Heads on the Dorset coast, the other — an equally superb viewpoint — situated further east. Offshore is a series of limestone rocks; from east to west: the Bull, Blind Cow, Cow and Calf.*

Just over the brow your next objective, the **Bat's Head** promontory with its natural arch comes into view, a chalk stack in the foreground. Carry on downhill, then up again to the top, where a **detour** (with care) out onto the headland provides *magnificent views in*

*either direction: Swyre Head and Durdle Door to the east, White Nothe to the west***.**

Carrying on, the **Coast Path** descends to **Middle Bottom**, then heads on uphill again passing the lower of a **pair of obelisk-like navigation beacons**. Continue (for about 370 metres) to the next junction.

3. Leaving the **Coast Path**, turn right along a path signed for 'Dagger's Gate', which leads to a junction with a bridleway and an information panel about **Chaldon Down**. Turn right along the grass, soon beside the fence on the left, continuing through the next two fields, ignoring a junction (not marked on the OS map) indicating 'East Chaldon' to the left and the 'Warren and Coast Path' to the right.

4. Go through a bridle gate (noting the waymarks on the post alongside) into a third field. Take the right fork maintaining direction and height, heading

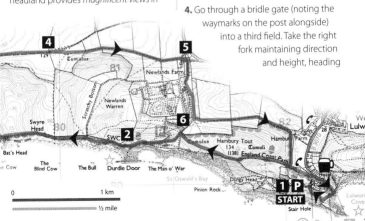

Lulworth Cove is part of the 'Jurassic Coast' — a World Heritage Site

towards some scrub by a fence. Continue along the grass to the right of the scrub. After a turning on the right for 'Scratchy Bottom', the path, now a track, reaches **Newlands Farm**.

5. Turn right along the private road and right again down the road to the **Durdle Door Holiday Park**. Where the road forks just past the **turning area**, branch off to the left along an attractive, new path (not shown on the OS map) signed for 'Durdle Door' that runs through the belt of trees on the eastern side of the Park.

6. Exit the woodland through a gate and turn left signed for 'West Lulworth'. The path heads gently downhill beside a fence on the left. At the next junction turn right for 'Lulworth Cove & car park', turning left to retrace your initial steps to the latter. To view **Lulworth Cove** and **Stair Hole**, continue to the road and turn right down to the cove. Turn right in front of the **Boat Shed Café** up steps, at the top of which, just over to the left is a fine view of the cove, with an Information panel nearby. The path continues up the coastal grassland to a **memorial stone** commemorating the inauguration of the Jurassic Coast as a World Heritage Site. Above it is a viewpoint overlooking **Stair Hole**. Turn right and follow the path to another **viewpoint** and **interpretation panel**, *which explains how erosion shapes*

the coast, creating caves, blow-holes, arches, stacks and stumps.

The Lulworth Crumple, as it is known — once flat sedimentary beds lifted up and tilted to form striking patterns — is very visible on either side of the cove.

Turn right at the road back to the main road and car park to complete the walk. ♦

Durdle Door

Durdle Door and Lulworth Cove are two of the most iconic geological features of the Jurassic coast — and both real crowd-pullers. Durdle Door's name comes from the Old English word 'thirl' meaning 'holed' or 'pierced'. As the nearby interpretation panel explains, there are five types of rock exposed in the cliffs here, chalk being the most obvious as you look westwards, while the famous Durdle Door arch is of Portland stone — a type of hard limestone.

The Castle Inn is an authentic thatched Dorset pub

Castle Inn
West Lulworth

What to expect:
Good downland paths and tracks, with some steep ups and downs

Distance/time: 10.25 kilometres / 6½ miles. Allow 3 - 3½ hours

Start: Lulworth Cove car park (charge)

Grid ref: SY 822 800

Ordnance Survey map: OS Explorer OL15 (Purbeck & South Dorset)

The Pub: Castle Inn, Main Road, West Lulworth, Wareham BH20 5RN | 01929 400311 | www.castleinn-lulworth.co.uk

Walk outline: This section of the South West Coast Path passes through the Lulworth Army Firing Ranges, where public access is restricted to specific times. Range walks include a spectacular stretch of the the Coast Path, plus inland paths and access to Tyneham village; all clearly marked. This walk can be shortened or extended, as wished.
Lulworth Range walks - access: Open every weekend throughout the year (except for 6), plus school holidays and bank holidays.

Just up from Lulworth Cove at the foot of Bindon Hill is the recently refurbished Castle Inn, a traditional 16th century picture postcard thatched pub.

Daily specials board

► The Castle Inn at a glance

Open: Daily noon-11pm
Brewery/company: Butcombe Brewery
Ales and wine: Butcombe beers, including Original and Rare Breed, plus guest ales; selection of ciders and interesting wines
Food: Plenty of choice from pub classics to Sunday roast; locally sourced seasonal produce. Children's menu. Food served daily noon-9pm
Accommodation: 12 charming bedrooms including 6 dog-friendly ones
Outside: Tables in front of the pub; terraced gardens at rear with views
Children & dogs: Both very welcome

The Walk

1. Exit the **car park**, cross the road and turn left along the access road that runs parallel to and above the main road, continuing on the roadside path towards West Lulworth. Take the first right, **Bindon Road**, and after 80 metres turn right and take the left of the two paths signed for the 'Range Walks', heading uphill then bearing left to a fence. Turn right up to the top of hill. This western end of **Bindon Hill** is access land (ie: you can walk anywhere), open at all times.

2. Go left through the gate — Range boundary — and continue eastwards along the **crest of Bindon Hill**, keeping left at the first fork. Lulworth Camp and the tank ranges are over to your left. At the eastern end of Bindon Hill you join up with the route of the **South West Coast Path**. There is a superb view over the cove of **Arish Mell** below with

Worbarrow Bay beyond, before a steep descent to the former (not open to the public). To shorten the walk carry on from Point 5 here.

3. Continuing on the **Coast Path** it's a steep climb up to the Iron Age hill fort known as **Flower's Barrow** where there's an **information panel**. *The splendid views well repay the exertion. Worbarrow Bay below (open to the public) is a lovely spot. There was once a coastal hamlet at Worbarrow, but, like Tyneham, it was evacuated during the Second World War.*

Tyneham's story is a poignant one. In 1943 its inhabitants were evacuated so the army could use the area as a firing range. The villagers assumed they would return but the land was requisitioned for permanent army use. Yet, decades of MoD control have kept development and intensive farming at bay.

4. The main route turns back here, but for those with the time and stamina, the

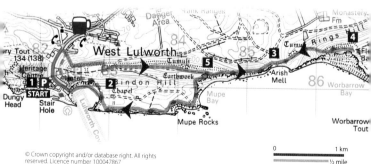

A superb view over Arish Mell cove to Worbarrow Bay and the Tout

walk can easily be extended. Head back down to Arish Mell and then back up the eastern end of Bindon Hill.

5. Where the path divides, go left on the **Coast Path** descending steeply to **Mupe Bay**. Thereafter continue on the Coast Path towards Lulworth Cove. Note the fascinating **Fossil Forest** before you exit the Ranges through another gate. The official Coast Path route involves more ascent and descent (and will bring you out at Bindon Road, from where you retrace your steps) but at most states of the tide you can avoid this by walking along the beach at Lulworth Cove, then back up the road to the car park, to complete the walk. ♦

Fossil forest

Situated to the east of Lulworth Cove in the Lulworth Ranges are the remains of an ancient submerged forest from the Jurassic period. When sea levels dropped, a tropical forest grew up and later flooded. The trees' stumps, trunks and roots were preserved by calcareous sediment deposited by freshwater algae. Today you can still see the doughnut-shaped fossilised 'tufa' or growth of algae which surrounded the trunks at the time.

The spacious, historic Scott Arms is popular with both locals and visitors

Scott Arms
Kingston

Distance/time: 8.25 kilometres / 5¼ miles. Allow 3 hours

Start: Houns-tout car park, Kingston

Grid ref: SY 953 794

Ordnance Survey map: OS Explorer OL15 (Purbeck & South Dorset)

The Pub: The Scott Arms, West Street, Kingston, Corfe Castle, Dorset BH20 5LH, (01929 480270), www.thescottarms.com

What to expect:
Good paths and tracks with one fairly steep ascent; stretch along quiet country lane

Walk outline: An easy, level walk to the coast through woodland and over open grassland to Houns-tout Cliff. Joining the Coast Path, the walk heads west down grassy slopes and steps to cross a wooded valley, continuing to Rope Lake Head where a permissive path leads inland to Swyre Head — another splendid viewpoint. From here it's an easy walk along the top to a quiet lane back to Kingston.

Roughly 1½ miles inland from the coast, the 18th century Kingston Arms boasts probably the best view of any pub over the Purbeck countryside, with Corfe Castle visible in the distance. Listed in the Good Pub Guide, it has a well deserved reputation. Events include popular Caribbean nights.

View from the beer garden

▶ The Scott Arms at a glance

Open: Daily from 11am
Brewery/company: Greene King
Ales and wine: Fine selection of ales (including Dorset Brewing Company's Jurassic Real Ale), ciders and wine
Food: Pub classics and seasonal specials; Caribbean barbecue on summer weekends. Served noon-2.30pm and 6-8pm, all day at weekends
Accommodation: Four attractively decorated en-suite double bedrooms
Outside: Wonderful view from large garden at rear towards Corfe Castle and Purbeck Hills with lots of tables for al fresco meals and drinks
Children & dogs: Both welcome

The Walk

1. From the **car park** head along the track through the **plantation** signed to the 'Coast Path and Houns-tout'. *In spring, bluebells and wild garlic border the route.* Beyond a stile and gate lies open grassland. The route continues ahead beside a wall on the left. *Over to the right is the Encombe valley where Encombe House, a privately owned Grade II listed country house built in 1735, is situated amongst the trees.*

Keeping over to the right of the hillside affords a better view down to the valley. Looking back to your right you will see an **obelisk** on the hilltop across the valley.

The house was formerly the seat of the Earls of Eldon and the obelisk was erected by the first Earl to commemorate his elder brother, Sir William Scott, becoming Baron Stowell.

2. A **stone bench** is situated atop **Houns-tout Cliff**, a splendid viewpoint. *Below to the east is Chapman's Pool, the flat-topped headland of St Aldhelm's Head beyond, while to the west the view stretches along the grassy-topped cliffs to distant Portland.*

Turn right to follow the **Coast Path** downhill, descending fairly steeply. **Steps** lead down through woodland to cross a valley, the path continuing uphill the other side and then along the undulating

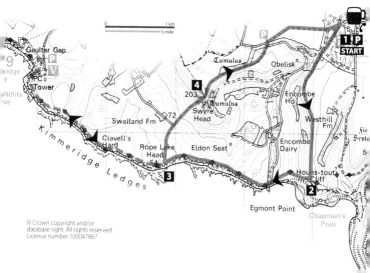

Looking west along the coast from Houns-tout Cliff

coastline — with fine views looking back to the east — to **Rope Lake Head**, where there is a **stone waymark**, signed for 'Swyre Head', and a stile on the right.

The walk turns inland here, but for those with the time and energy, a 3-mile out-and-back extension is recommended.

Walk extension: Continuing along the undulating Coast Path for another 1½ miles will take you to the **Clavell Tower**, a notable landmark, and, just beyond, a fine view over **Kimmeridge Bay**.

Optional inland return: Instead of returning the same way, you could continue round the bay and then follow the path inland through fields to **Kimmeridge Village**, *where you will find the Etches Collection – Museum of Jurassic Marine Life. This remarkable collection of marine fossils is named after Steve Etches, a local fossil collector and expert who has spent over 35 years scouring the rocks in the area, discovering over 2,500 fossils. Also in the village is Clavell's Restaurant serving lunches and afternoon tea.*

Enjoy extensive views along the coast from the top of Swyre Head

To continue, follow the path up past the **churchyard**, rejoining the road at a junction. Cross and follow the lane opposite, soon forking right along a ridge-top track over **Smedmore Hill** that leads to **Swyre Head**, where you rejoin the main route at Point 4. This alternative return is about 1 mile longer.

3. Otherwise, for the **main route**, turn right and follow the permissive path inland, with the fence on your left. At a gate continue along the farm track, then the path, to another gate, bearing left to cross a stile. The path continues up the right hand side of the field to a further gate.

The last short section is the steepest, but the views from the top of **Swyre Head** well repay the effort. *At 203 metres above sea level, this is the highest point in Purbeck, but the impressive* **tumulus** *here adds to the height. It's worth walking to the far end beyond it to make the most of the views.*

4. With the fence to your right head northwards across the grass along the rim of the valley, Encombe now below to the right, curving round to the right to continue alongside **Polar Wood** on the left. Go through the bridle gate and carry on along the track that leads across a field to a **car park** and lane. Turn right, back to the start, to complete the walk. ♦

The imposing Victorian Church of St James stands proudly above Kingston village. Resembling a miniature cathedral, it is unusually large for such a small village. The third Earl of Eldon had the church built *in the late 1870s, employing the architect, George Edmund Street, who specialised in the Gothic Revival style.*

Clavell Tower, Kimmeridge

The four-storey circular tower was built in 1830 by the Reverend John Richards Clavell of Smedmore House as an observatory and folly. With the tower threatened by coastal erosion, in 2006 the Landmark Trust relocated it 25 metres inland from the cliff edge. The project, supported by the Heritage Lottery Fund, involved carefully dismantling and re-erecting it. Today, this cliff-top retreat is let out to holiday-makers by the Trust.

Stone seats and tables on the green in front of the Square and Compass, Worth Matravers

Square & Compass
Worth Matravers

Distance/time: 8.5 kilometres / 5½ miles. Allow 3 hours. (Alternative longer route via Dancing Ledge, 12 kilometres /7½ miles)

Start: Village car park, Worth Matravers (small charge)

Grid ref: SY 974 776

Ordnance Survey map: OS Explorer OL15 (Purbeck & South Dorset)

The Pub: Square & Compass, Worth Matravers, Swanage BH19 3LF | 01929 439229 | www.squareandcompasspub.co.uk

What to expect:
Good paths, grassy terrain; Coast Path and field paths; one steep ascent and descent

Walk outline: From the village the walk heads down Seacombe Bottom valley to the Coast Path, turning right to follow it clockwise round St Aldhelm's Head past the quarry caves at Winspit. Continuing on the west side of the headland, after a steep descent and corresponding ascent, it's easy walking along Emmetts Hill and back inland to Worth. An alternative longer route takes in Dancing Ledge, a former quarry and popular landmark on the Purbeck coast.

Full of character, unpretentious and popular with locals and visitors alike, the 18th century Square & Compass has two simple rooms with flagstones and a wood burner; drinks are served through a hatch rather than at a bar.

Quarrymen's pub?

▶ The Square & Compass at a glance

Open: Noon – 11pm daily
Company/brewery: Free house
Ales and wine: Choice of locally brewed beers from Hattie Brown's Brewery, as well as guest ales. Ciders include home-pressed traditional cider made by the owner
Food: Selection of tasty, hot, home-made pasties and pies with a variety of fillings, available at all times
Outside: Plenty of seating with sea views
Children & dogs: Both welcome

The Walk

1. Turn right out of the **car park** and at the T-junction bear right down to the **village pond** forking left in front of it. Almost immediately turn left, ignore the next left and continue down the no through access road signed for 'Seacombe', very shortly turning left along a **raised footpath** beside a wall parallel to a drive below. Go through a gate and continue ahead across the grass, maintaining direction as the path dips and rises. After crossing a **stone stile** the path descends to a kissing gate. Note the ridges in the hillsides known as strip lynchets, cut in medieval times to provide extra arable land. Steps lead down from the gate towards the valley below. The path levels out along **Seacombe Bottom** joining the **Coast Path** before reaching the coast itself.

2. Turn right up steps through vegetation to emerge on the open **grassy cliff-top**. Heading on south-westwards there's a fine view back towards distant Anvil Point and its lighthouse.

In about 1 kilometre, the **Coast Path** goes through a gate ('National Trust East Man' sign on the other side) and descends steps to the **Winspit valley** reaching a T-junction with a broad track. A short detour along to the left takes you to the remains of the **old stone quarry** and **quarry caves**.

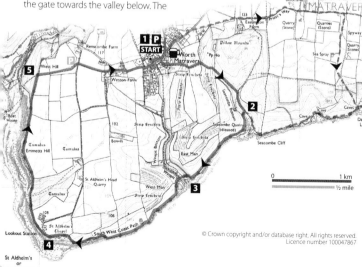

The curious Norman chapel on St Aldhelm's Head

3. Retrace your steps to the junction and continue along the **Coast Path** which turns left up steps back onto the cliff-top, with a good view over the quarry below. A steady climb takes you up to the **top of St Aldhelm's Head** passing a **radar memorial** sculpture.

This commemorates the pioneering work on radar undertaken at Worth Matravers during the Second World War between 1940 and 1942; it played a crucial role in winning the war. Nothing remains of the original huge aerials and buildings, which were removed after the war.

Just beyond is the **National Coastwatch Institution lookout**, manned by volunteers, and behind that **St Aldhelm's Chapel**.

The isolated chapel, dedicated to St Aldhelm, first Bishop of Sherborne, is a striking square building. Given its location, it is thought it may have served as a marker for seafarers, too. Of Norman origin, it was restored in the 19th century having fallen into disrepair. Look inside to see the fine vaulted roof.

4. Continuing along the top from the lookout station you soon reach a **stone**

Overlooking Chapman's Pool and Houns-tout Cliff from Emmets Hill

bench and a splendid view north-westwards along the coastline. The path then heads on down quite steeply and back up again (steps each side) to the top of **Emmetts Hill**, where it carries on along the level. *There are some superb views over Chapman's Pool with Houns-tout Cliff beyond.* About 750 metres along you'll come to a **memorial** with a stone table and benches in memory of the Royal Marines who have lost their lives since World War II. A little further on is a **stone waymark** and stile on the right.

5. Leave the **Coast Path** turning right here and follow the path across fields to a **car park**. Cross the access road and go through the gate opposite continuing along the field edge path to **Weston Farm**, bearing left to the lane. Turn right back to **Worth**, following the road round to the left to pass the Norman **church of St Nicholas** — worth a look inside.

Alternative longer route via Dancing Ledge

Turn right out of the **car park** and at the T-junction go left past the pub and follow the road out of the village. After 370 metres fork right through a gate across the field, cross a track and continue in the same direction across fields to join a track — the **Priest's Way**. Continue along this for a little under a mile to a **waymark**

stone on the left, signed 'Footpath to Dancing Ledge'. Go right through the gate opposite and at the fork bear left continuing along the left side of the field to another gate. Go through this and head down to the **coast** and **Dancing Ledge**.

The cliffs above the ledge are popular with climbers. The pool was created for school swimming. Turn right along the **Coast Path** joining the main route at **Seacombe**, at Point 2, to complete the walk. ♦

Winspit Quarry caves

Winspit is a disused quarry on the cliffs south of Worth Matravers. The caves here were created by the quarrying of stone, which was used for many of the major buildings in London. Quarrying continued until the Second World War, when the site was used for naval and air defences. After the war, the caves were opened to the public. The quarry has been used as a film location for television series Doctor Who and Blake's 7 and is popular with climbers.

The 16th century Bankes Arms in Studland village

Bankes Arms
Studland

What to expect:
Good paths and tracks along cliff-tops, downland ridge and heath, short stretches along roadside

Distance/time: 10 kilometres / 6¼ miles. Allow 3-3½ hours

Start: NT South Beach car park, Studland

Grid ref: SZ 037 825

Ordnance Survey map: OS Explorer OL15 (Purbeck & South Dorset)

The Pub: The Bankes Arms, Manor Road, Studland BH19 3AU | 01929 450225 | www.bankesarms.com

Walk outline: From the car park an easy initial stretch along the Coast Path leads to Handfast Point and Old Harry Rocks. Continuing on the grassy cliff-top, it's a gradual climb to Ballard Point, from where the route heads westwards along the top of Ballard Down. The return leg crosses Godlingston Heath, a National Nature Reserve, passing the Agglestone rock, to finish at Studland's interesting Norman church.

The 16th century Bankes Arms is just a short stroll from the beach and close to the iconic chalk sea stacks of Old Harry Rocks. In front of the pub just across the road is an extensive garden with plenty of seating and uninterrupted sea views.

Spacious bar

▶ The Bankes Arms at a glance

Open: Daily 11am-11pm (10.30pm on Sunday)

Brewery/company: Free house

Ales and wine: Choice of beers from pub's own award-winning Isle of Purbeck Brewery, plus guest ales and cider; good selection of wines

Food: Varied menu from bar snacks and pub favourites to gourmet dishes, often locally sourced. Served noon-3pm and 6-9pm, Mon-Thurs; noon-9.30pm Fri & Sat, noon-9pm on Sun. In summer, daily noon-9.30pm

Accommodation: 9 bedrooms, most en-suite, some with sea views

Children & dogs: Both welcome **Outside:** Pub garden with sea views

The Walk

1. Turn right out of the **car park** past the **Bankes Arms** and walk down the road, turning left at the **public toilets** along a track/bridleway, the route of the **South West Coast Path**. This leads to **Handfast Point** and the chalk stacks of **Old Harry Rocks**, one of Dorset's most famous landmarks. *The headland marks the eastern end of the Jurassic coast and is the youngest in geological time. Across the water to the east the Needles on the Isle of Wight can be seen; these are part of the same chalk band, which once joined the latter to the mainland. From here there are also far-reaching views across Poole Bay.*

2. Continuing along the grassy cliff-top **Coast Path** two more chalk stacks, the **Pinnacles**, are passed below. A gradual ascent leads to **Ballard Point** — at the first gate, where a bridleway forks right, keep to the cliff-top path. Go through the next gate and head to the **trig point**. *The extensive views from here take in Swanage Bay to the south and Poole Harbour to the north.*

3. Carry on westwards along the top of the grassy **Ballard Down** ridge (ignore crossing paths), in due course going through a gate and descending to an **obelisk**. *This commemorates the provision of a new supply of drinking water for Swanage in 1883. It was taken down in 1941 to avoid it being used as a landmark by enemy aircraft in the war, but later rebuilt.*

Old Harry Rocks are constantly eroded by the sea

4. Keep ahead along the bridleway which becomes a chalky track that curves right and descends to a gate and the road. Cross and turn left along the verge, then turn right after 250 metres at a footpath sign and stile. Follow the path uphill across the grass and through some **woodland** to a **golf course**. A waymark post indicates the direction to take, leading to another stile and road. Turn briefly left to a bridleway on the right. Go through the gate and follow the path, keeping ahead at both bridleway junctions soon reached — signed for 'Agglestone and Studland Heath' on the **waymark stones**. Bear left at the next fork — the right one for golfers only. The path leads down through gorse and heather to a gate and junction beyond. Continue ahead, before long descending to the **Agglestone Rock** visible below, from where there are fine views over the heath to Poole harbour. *The 17-foot high, 400-tonne block is a remnant of a band of iron-rich sandstone which once covered the heath.*

5. Steps lead down the other side of the rock, with stretches of **boardwalk**

A summer dawn illuminates the Old Harry Rocks

along the path across the heath beyond. When the path forks bear right, and soon bear right again and again after that at a **waymark post** among the trees, where a bridleway joins from the left. Continue on the bridleway crossing a **footbridge,** and then along a rough access road past dwellings. At the next bridleway intersection turn right through the trees and left at the next junction. Keep ahead ignoring turnings either side, eventually reaching **Heath Green Road**. Turn left to the **crossroads**, go straight across down **School Lane**, and soon take a footpath on the left signed to the 'church'.

Built on the site of an earlier Saxon church,

St Nicholas is a Romanesque Norman building with a low solid tower above the chancel. There is much of interest both inside and out. The church is notable for its corbel table carvings, amongst which are some grotesque and quasi-erotic ones.

A path leads from here back to the nearby **car park** to complete the walk. ♦

To learn more about Studland's role during World War Two and to see some of the defences, a short, easy extension is recommended. Across the road from the car park, follow the Coast Path signed for 'Fort Henry'. The path leads to the coast and then northwards to Redend Point and Fort Henry, a concrete observation bunker.

In 1944 it was used by Churchill, Eisenhower and King George VI to watch rehearsals for D-Day. There is a fine view of Studland beach from here. The long sandy beach was ideal as a training site, while the uninhabited adjoining heath could be bombarded with live ammunition. Information panels provide more details. Retrace your steps to the car park, or continue to the beach and along it as far as you like.

Studland Bay

Studland Bay is part of the Bankes Estate donated to the National Trust in 1981. Its long sandy beach, dunes and heath are popular with visitors in summer. One section is a designated naturist zone. During the Second World War, Studland played an important role as a training area for troops preparing for D-Day. The South West Coast Path finishes its 630-mile journey north of here at South Haven Point, at the southern entrance to Poole Harbour.

Useful Information

South West Coast Path Association
A charity that champions the South West Coast Path, as well as helping fund path repairs and improvements. **www.southwestcoastpath.org.uk** | 01752 896237

Visit Dorset
Dorset's official tourism website covers everything needed to plan and book a holiday or short break in Dorset. **www.visit-dorset.com**

Jurassic Coast World Heritage Site
The Jurassic Coast website provides useful information about the World Heritage Site including its geology and fossils. **www.jurassiccoast.org**

Tourist Information Centres
The TICs provide free information and advice on everything from accommodation and transport to what's on and walking advice.

Lyme Regis	01297 442138
Bridport	01308 424901
Dorchester	01305 267992
Discover Purbeck (Wareham)	01929 552740
Swanage	01929 766018

Dorset Breweries and Pubs
As well as the main Dorset breweries Hall & Woodhouse (Badger Ales) of Blandford, and Palmers of Bridport, the county also supports a dozen microbreweries and producers of real ales and craft beers, plus a score of real cider and perry makers. For details of the encouragingly high number of real ale pubs in Dorset, see the local CAMRA websites, or buy a copy of their excellent annual Good Beer Guide. Visitors can also sample a superb range of local real ales at the many beer festivals held throughout the year.

See: **www.camra.org.uk** or **www.eastdorset.camra.org.uk** or **www.camrawdorset.org.uk**

Rail travel
Mainline railway stations at Bournemouth, Poole, Dorchester, Wareham and Weymouth. **www.thetrainline.com** or **www.nationalrail.co.uk** (03457 484950)

Bus travel
The Dorset coast is accessible by bus from various inland points with train connections, visit **www.travelinesw.com** | 0871 200 2233